Teaching Notes

Contents

This Is Me

Wheels

Dogs

Maya's Family

Making Muffins

Big and Little

Introduction

Fireflies is an exciting non-fiction series within *Oxford Reading Tree*. These books are specially designed to be used alongside the Stage 1+ stories. They provide practice of reading skills in a non-fiction context whilst using the same simple, repetitive sentence structures as the *Oxford Reading Tree* stories. They also contain a selection of decodable and tricky words. Each stage builds on the reading skills and vocabulary from previous stages. Each book offers scope for developing children's word recognition and language comprehension skills in a highly motivating way, whilst also providing strong cross-curricular links.

To help children approach each new book in this stage with confidence, you should prepare the children for reading by talking about the book and asking questions. You can use these *Teaching Notes* and the additional notes in the inside front and back covers of the pupil books to help you. The notes within the pupil books can also be used by parents or teaching assistants.

Using the books

This booklet provides suggestions for using the books for guided, group and independent activities. The reading activities include ideas for developing children's *word recognition* **W** and *language comprehension* **C** skills. Within word recognition, there are ideas for helping children practise their phonic skills and knowledge, as well as helping them tackle words which are not easy to decode phonically. The language comprehension ideas include suggestions for teaching the skills of prediction, questioning, clarifying, summarising and imagining, in order to help children understand the texts. Suggestions are also provided for speaking and listening and writing activities, as well as for introducing linked electronic material and cross-curricular links.

Reading fluency

To support children in developing fluency in their reading, you can give them plenty of opportunities to revisit the books. These include:

- rereading independently
- rereading with a partner
- rereading at home
- hearing the book read to them as they follow the printed text.

Rereading and rehearing helps children develop automatic word recognition and gives them models of fluent, expressive reading.

Comprehension strategies

Story	Comprehension strategy taught through these Teaching Notes				
	Prediction	Questioning	Clarifying	Summarising	Imagining
This Is Me	✓	✓	✓	✓	✓
Wheels	✓	✓	✓	✓	
Dogs	✓	✓	✓	✓	✓
Maya's Family	✓	✓	✓	✓	✓
Making Muffins	✓	✓	✓	✓	✓
Big and Little	✓	✓	✓	✓	✓

Vocabulary and phonic opportunities

The chart shows the main words used in each book. The decodable words listed should be decodable for most children at this Stage. The tricky words are common but do not conform to the phonic rules taught up to this point – children will need support to learn and recognise them. If children struggle with one of these words you can model how to read it.

This Is Me	High frequency decodable words	
	High frequency tricky words	this, is, my
Wheels	High frequency decodable words	
	High frequency tricky words	here, is, wheel, there, are
Dogs	High frequency decodable words	dog, at
	High frequency tricky words	this, is, look
Maya's Family	High frequency decodable words	am
	High frequency tricky words	this, is, her, I
Making Muffins	High frequency decodable words	in
	High frequency tricky words	I, put, the
Big and Little	High frequency decodable words	at, it, big
	High frequency tricky words	look, this, is, little

Curriculum coverage chart

	Speaking and listening	Reading	Writing
This Is Me			
PNS Literacy Framework (YF)	2.3	**W** 5.2, 5.9 **C** 5.1, 7.1, 7.3	9
National Curriculum	Working towards Level 1		
Scotland (5–14) (P1)	Level A	Level A	Level A
N. Ireland (P1/Y1)	Social use of language: 3, 5 Language and thinking: 3, 4, 5	1, 4, 5, 6, 7, 8, 11	1, 2, 3
Wales (Key Stage 1)	Range: 1, 2, 3 Skills: 1, 2, 4	Range: 1, 2, 3 Skills: 1, 2	Range: 1, 3 Skills: 2, 3, 6
	Speaking and listening	Reading	Writing
Wheels			
PNS Literacy Framework (YF)	1.4	**W** 5.6, 5.8, 5.9 **C** 7.2, 7.3	9
National Curriculum	Working towards Level 1		
Scotland (5–14) (P1)	Level A	Level A	Level A
N. Ireland (P1/Y1)	Social use of language: 3, 5 Language and thinking: 7, 8, 9	1, 4, 5, 6, 7, 8, 11	3, 6
Wales (Key Stage 1)	Range: 1, 2, 3 Skills: 1, 2, 3, 4	Range: 1, 2, 3 Skills: 1, 2	Range: 1, 3, 4 Skills: 3, 6

Key

C = Language comprehension
W = Word recognition
Y = Year
F = Foundation
P = Primary
In the designations such as 5.2, the first number represents the strand and the second number the bullet point

Curriculum coverage chart

	Speaking and listening	Reading	Writing
Dogs			
PNS Literacy Framework (YF)	2.2	W 5.1, 5.2, 5.9 C 7.3	9
National Curriculum	Working towards Level 1		
Scotland (5–14) (P1)	Level A	Level A	Level A
N. Ireland (P1/Y1)	Social use of language: 3, 5 Language and thinking: 8, 9, 10	1, 4, 5, 6, 7, 8, 11	1, 2, 3, 4
Wales (Key Stage 1)	Range: 1, 2, 3 Skills: 1, 2, 3, 4	Range: 1, 2, 3 Skills: 1, 2	Range: 1, 3 Skills: 2, 3, 5
	Speaking and listening	**Reading**	**Writing**
Maya's Family			
PNS Literacy Framework (YF)	1.4	W 5.5, 5.9, 5.10 C 7.2	11
National Curriculum	Working towards Level 1		
Scotland (5–14) (P1)	Level A	Level A	Level A
N. Ireland (P1/Y1)	Social use of language: 3, 5 Language and thinking: 7, 8, 9	1, 4, 5, 7, 8, 11	1, 2, 3, 4
Wales (Key Stage 1)	Range: 1, 2, 3 Skills: 1, 2, 3, 5	Range: 1, 2, 3 Skills: 1, 2	Range: 1, 3 Skills: 2, 3

Curriculum coverage chart

	Speaking and listening	Reading	Writing
Making Muffins			
PNS Literacy Framework (YF)	2.2	(W) 5.6, 5.9 (C) 7.3	11
National Curriculum	Working towards Level 1		
Scotland (5–14) (P1)	Level A	Level A	Level A
N. Ireland (P1/Y1)	Social use of language: 3, 5 Language and thinking: 8, 10, 11	1, 4, 5, 6, 7, 8, 11	1, 2, 3, 4, 6
Wales (Key Stage 1)	Range: 1, 2, 3 Skills: 1, 2, 4	Range: 1, 2, 3 Skills: 1, 2	Range: 1, 3 Skills: 2, 3, 5
	Speaking and listening	**Reading**	**Writing**
Big and Little			
PNS Literacy Framework (YF)	3.1	(W) 5.2, 5.5, 5.9 (C) 7.2	9
National Curriculum	Working towards Level 1		
Scotland (5–14) (P1)	Level A	Level A	Level A
N. Ireland (P1)	Social use of language: 3, 4, 5 Language and thinking: 9, 10, 11	1, 4, 5, 6, 7, 8, 11	3, 6
Wales (Key Stage 1)	Range: 1, 2, 3 Skills: 1, 2, 3, 4	Range: 1, 2, 3 Skills: 1, 2	Range: 1, 3, 4 Skills: 3, 6

This Is Me

> **C** = Language comprehension   **R, AF** = QCA reading assessment focus
>
> **W** = Word recognition   **W, AF** = QCA writing assessment focus

Group or guided reading

Introducing the book

C *(Prediction)* Read the title, pointing to the words, and showing the picture. Ask: *Do you think this is a story, or a book that tells us about things?*

C *(Clarifying)* Look at some of the pictures and notice that this book is showing us facts, not a story.

Strategy check

Ask the children to show you where they will begin reading on the first page. Check that everyone points to the correct word.

Independent reading

- Ask children to read the book aloud. Praise and encourage them while they read, and prompt as necessary.

C *(Summarising)* Ask children to tell you about the picture on page 8. Praise them for explaining that the pictures on each page are jigsaw pieces, and that they all fit together to make a complete picture of the boy.

Assessment Check that children:

- *(R, AF1)* track text, matching letters to sounds
- *(R, AF1)* use phonic knowledge to sound out and blend the phonemes in words, particularly the phonic words (see chart on page 4)
- *(R, AF2)* can relate the information in the book to their own bodies.

Returning to the text

(c) *(Summarising)* What do all the picture pieces make on the last page? Does every jigsaw piece show a part of the boy?

(c) *(Questioning)* Ask children to find a particular body part, e.g. *Where is the page that shows his hair?* Ask them to trace the arrow from the text to the right part of the picture.

(c) *(Imagining)* Ask children to say what could be shown on other pages if the book were bigger.

Group and independent reading activities

Objective   Know that print carries meaning and in English is read from left to right (7.1).

(W) Ask the children to find the title on the front cover. Read it together, pointing to 'This' first. On each page ask the children to point to the first word before beginning to read. Notice that each sentence begins with 'This'.

Assessment   *(R, AF1)* Did the children automatically point to the first word on the left of each page?

Objective   Read some high frequency words (5.9).

(W) Ask the children to find and read the word 'is' on page 2. Look for 'is' on each page, then count the number of times 'is' appears in the book. Repeat with 'This' and 'my'.

Assessment   *(R, AF1)* Can children find the words 'is', 'this' and 'my' in a collection of flashcards, or in a different story?

Objective   Link sounds to letters, naming and sounding the letters of the alphabet (5.2).

(W) Ask the children to find the first letter of the word 'nose' on page 3. Ask them to say the letter name and the sound. Think of another word that begins with 'n'. Repeat with 'hair' (page 4) and 'tongue' (page 5).

Assessment   *(R, AF1)* Can the children name and say the sounds of the letters?

Objective Show understanding of ways that information can be found in non-fiction texts (7.3).

C *(Questioning)* Ask children to find particular body parts in the book, e.g. *Find the word 'tongue'. How do you know that you are right?*

Assessment *(R, AF2)* Can the children find the right picture, and the matching word?

Objective Explore and experiment with sounds, words and texts (5.1).

C *(Clarifying)* Write these incomplete sentences on a board or large sheet of paper, with the list of words:

is my hand.	This
This is my	eye.
This is tongue.	my
This my nose.	is

Read the sentences together and ask the children to say which word from the list is needed to complete each sentence.

Assessment *(R, AF2)* Could the children find the missing words and make the sentences make sense?

Speaking and listening activities

Objective Extend their vocabulary, exploring the meanings and sounds of new words (2.3).

- Ask the children to sit in a circle. Take turns around the circle to say 'This is my...' and name a body part. Encourage children to name less obvious parts, such as knuckles, wrists, nostrils.

- If children find this easy, make it cumulative, mentioning all the parts children have pointed to so far, and adding one, pointing and saying, e.g. *This is my nose, my eyebrow, my knee, and my shoulder.*

Cross-curricular links: Early Years Foundation Stage

Knowledge and Understanding of the World:

- Identify features of living things.
  Look closely at similarities and differences.

Writing activities

Objective Attempt writing for various purposes, using features of different forms (9).

Ask the children to draw a large picture of themselves. Show them how to draw label lines and write the name of the body part that the line indicates.

Assessment *(W, AF2)* Could the children write at least three or four words to label their picture?

Wheels

> **C** = Language comprehension   *R, AF* = QCA reading assessment focus
>
> **W** = Word recognition   *W, AF* = QCA writing assessment focus

Group or guided reading

Introducing the book

C *(Clarifying)* Read the title, and ask the children to say what they can see in the picture. Count the wheels and say how many bicycles there are.

C *(Prediction)* Read the blurb on the back cover, and ask the children to say what they think will be in this book.

Strategy check

Remind the children to point to each word as they read.

Independent reading

Ask children to read the book aloud. Praise and encourage them while they read, and prompt as necessary.

C *(Questioning, Summarising)* Ask: *What did you count in this book? What was in the pictures?*

Assessment Check that children:

- *(R, AF1)* track text, pointing to each word as they say it
- *(R, AF1)* use letter sounds as clues to new words
- *(R, AF2)* use comprehension skills to predict the text.

Returning to the text

C *(Questioning, Clarifying)* Ask: *Did you notice that the pictures were in order? Can you explain the order? How many wheels should come after page 7?*

C *(Questioning)* Ask children to show you a page with three wheels.

C *(Summarising)* Close the book and ask the children to tell you what this book is about.

Group and independent reading activities

Objective Read some high frequency words (5.9).

(W) Notice that the number words are in a different colour in the sentence. Find the same number word in the caption to the picture. Make cards with number words for one to six. Ask the children to match each number word to the right picture. Practise reading the number words on cards in numerical order, and in random order.

Assessment *(R, AF1)* Could the children read the number words on sight?

Objective Recognise common digraphs (5.8).

Read simple words by sounding out and blending the phonemes all through the word from left to right (5.6).

(W) Find and read the word 'Wheels' on the front cover. Notice that 'wh' makes the 'w' sound. Ask the children to find 'wh' as often as they can in the book. Segment the phonemes in 'wheels' (wh–ee–l–s) and say them slowly together. Write the phonemes on a board as you say them. Then blend the sounds to say the whole word.

Assessment *(R, AF1)* Could the children find the digraph 'wh' on several pages? Could they segment and then blend the phonemes in 'wheels' with help?

Objective Extend their vocabulary, exploring the meanings and sounds of words (7.2).

(W) Ask the children to tell you the names of parts of a bicycle, e.g. seat, handlebars, chain, mudguards, spokes, tyres. Make a list of the children's suggestions. Look at each picture in turn and find as many parts from the list as you can.

Assessment *(R, AF1)* Did the children understand and use the new vocabulary?

Objective Show understanding of ways that information can be found in non-fiction texts (7.3).

(C) *(Questioning)* Talk about the order in which the pictures are arranged in the book. Ask: *Will a picture of one wheel come near the beginning or near the end of the book? Where will a picture of six wheels be? Can you guess which numbers are in the middle of the book?* Find the middle pages of the book to check. Look at the page numbers. Ask the children to find the first page, the last page and the middle pages.

Assessment *(R, AF2)* Did the children understand the sequence of the book? Could they use that knowledge to find the location of particular facts?

Objective Show understanding of ways that information can be found in non-fiction texts (7.3).

C *(Questioning, Clarifying)* Copy sentences from the book on to strips of paper. Use an incorrect sentence strip to cover the existing text on any page. Read the new sentence together and ask: *Does this make sense?* Ask the children to explain what is wrong, and to find and read the correct sentence for that page.

Assessment *(R, AF2)* Can children say how they knew that a sentence didn't make sense?

E-links

Fireflies Plus

If you are an Espresso user, you can access videos, quizzes and activities linked to this title to enrich your children's reading. Children can also write, post and compare reviews of the book. Full supporting Teaching Notes for this content are available on the site in PDF format. Within the Espresso site, follow the route **<Channel guide → English 1 → Oxford Reading Tree Fireflies Plus logo>**. *Espresso Primary* is an extensive library of cross-curricular, video-rich broadband teaching resources and learning activities that motivates children and supports teachers.

Speaking and listening activities

Objective Speak clearly and audibly with confidence and control and show awareness of the listener (1.4).

● Describe a vehicle to the children without saying the name, telling them the number of wheels, the number of people who can travel in it and what it is for. The children guess the name of the vehicle. The first person to guess correctly has the next turn at describing a vehicle. They may need to be prompted by questions, e.g. *How many wheels? What is it for? How many people can go in it or on it?* Praise children for successfully describing and guessing each vehicle.

Cross-curricular links: Early Years Foundation Stage

Problem Solving, Reasoning and Numeracy

- Say and use number names in order in familiar contexts.
  Count reliably up to ten everyday objects.

Writing activities

Objective Attempt writing for various purposes, using features of different forms (9).

- Explain that a Contents page in a book tells us what is on each page. Show the children how to write a Contents page, beginning like this:

Contents	
One wheel	page 2
Two wheels	page 3

Complete the Contents page as a shared writing activity, or ask the children to continue independently.

Assessment *(W, AF2)* Did the children understand how to write a Contents page? Did they tell the teacher what to write next, or write it themselves?

Dogs

> **C** = Language comprehension
> **W** = Word recognition
>
> **R, AF** = QCA reading assessment focus
> **W, AF** = QCA writing assessment focus

Group or guided reading

Introducing the book

C *(Imagining)* Read the title and talk about the picture. Ask the children to say where the dogs seem to be, and what they are doing. Ask: *Where do you think the dogs' owners are?*

C *(Prediction)* Read the blurb on the back cover. Ask the children to say what dogs can do. Ask: *What are the dogs on the front cover doing?* Ask them to predict what dogs might be doing in the pictures in this book.

Strategy check

Make sure that the children know where the book begins and where to begin reading each sentence.

Independent reading

● Ask children to read the book aloud. Praise and encourage them while they read, and prompt as necessary.

C *(Summarising)* Ask children to tell you whether this is a story about dogs, or a book that tells us what dogs can do.

Assessment Check that children:

● *(R, AF1)* track text, reading each word as they point to it

● *(R, AF1)* use phonic knowledge to work out and predict words that are new to them

● *(R, AF2)* use comprehension skills to work out what is happening in each picture.

Returning to the text

C *(Questioning)* Ask: *Which dog is eating? Which dog is running?* Ask the children to tell you the page number for each answer.

(C) *(Clarifying)* Ask the children to find dogs that are wet. Ask: *How did they get wet?*

(C) *(Summarising)* Ask the children to recall and tell you the six things that dogs in this book can do. Use the glossary page to check that they are correct.

Group and independent reading activities

Objective Link sounds and letters, naming and sounding letters (5.2).

(W) Use page 8. Look at the first picture. Ask what the dog is doing. Ask the children to tell you the name of the letter that 'sleeping' begins with. Ask: *What is the letter sound?* Find and name the second letter, 'l'. Say the two sounds separately, then blend them together. Then say the whole word, 'sleeping'.

● Repeat with 'swimming'. If the children are finding this easy, continue to look at the next three words in the same way. Before looking at 'eating,' explain that 'e' and 'a' together make the 'ee' sound. Do not attempt to sound the letters separately.

Assessment *(R, AF1)* Were the children able to name and sound the first two letters of the words you looked at? Could they blend the letters and hear them at the beginning of each word?

Objective Read some high frequency words (5.9).

(W) Check that the children can read 'is' and 'at' on sight. Ask them to find and read each word as often as they can in this book. Sharp-eyed children will also find them on the back cover. Ask them to look for 'this' anywhere in the book. Ask each child to point to and read the word they have found. Notice that sometimes it has a capital letter: 'This'. Talk about using capital letters for the first word in any sentence. Then ask the children to find 'Look' and count the number of times it appears in the book. Make word cards with: 'Look', 'This', 'this', 'at' and 'is'. Ask the children to read the words in random order.

Assessment *(R, AF1)* Could the children read the high frequency words: 'Look', 'This', 'this', 'is', 'at'?

Objective Explore and experiment with sounds, words and texts (5.1).

W Make four cards with the words: 'eating', 'sleeping', 'jumping' and 'fetching'. Read the four words and notice that they all end with 'ing'. Choose one card and ask the children to find the page in the book with that word. Ask them to cover the 'ing' part of the word. Help them to read the remaining word, i.e. 'eat', 'sleep', 'jump' or 'fetch'. Ask them to tell you some more things that dogs can do, e.g. walk, scratch, play, bark. Make a list of the suggestions. Ask the children to tell you how to change 'walk' to 'walking'. Write the new word. Repeat with other suggestions.

Assessment (R, AF1) Did the children understand that some words can be changed by adding 'ing'?

Objective Show understanding about how information can be found in non-fiction texts (7.3).

C (Questioning) Explain that a glossary shows what words in a book mean. Look at page 8, and read the words 'Picture Glossary'. Talk about the way the picture shows us what the word means. Use page 8 as a quiz page. Ask children in turn to ask the others to find the page with a particular action word, e.g. *Find the word 'eating'*. The other children find the page, and then one of them becomes the person to tell the children what to find next.

Assessment (R, AF2) Did the children understand that every word in the Glossary appeared somewhere else in the book?

E-links

Fireflies Plus

If you are an Espresso user, you can access videos, quizzes and activities linked to this title to enrich your children's reading. Children can also write, post and compare reviews of the book. Full supporting Teaching Notes for this content are available on the site in PDF format. Within the Espresso site, follow the route **<Channel guide → English 1 → Oxford Reading Tree Fireflies Plus logo>**. *Espresso Primary* is an extensive library of cross-curricular, video-rich broadband teaching resources and learning activities that motivates children and supports teachers.

Speaking and listening activities

Objective Sustain attentive listening, responding to what they have heard by relevant comments, questions or actions (2.2).

- Ask the children to say which of the dogs in the book they like best. Ask them to say what they like about the dog and whether they know a dog like it. Ask them to listen to each other, and find out if one of the dogs in the book is more popular than any of the others. You could keep a tally to see how often each dog is chosen.

Cross-curricular links: Early Years Foundation Stage

Knowledge and Understanding of the World

- Find out about, and identify, some features of living things. Look closely at similarities, differences, patterns and change.

Writing activities

Objective Attempt writing for various purposes (9).

Use the list of things that dogs can do from the group's activity suggestions, or ask the children to make suggestions now. Make a list of the words. Ask each child to draw a dog performing one of the actions. Help them to write the action word themselves. Some children may be able to write the whole sentence: 'This dog is...'. Use the pages to make a class book for everyone to read.

Assessment *(W, AF2)* Could the children tell you what their dog was doing and attempt to write the word?

Maya's Family

> **C** = Language comprehension **R, AF** = QCA reading assessment focus
>
> **W** = Word recognition **W, AF** = QCA writing assessment focus

Group or guided reading

Introducing the book

C *(Prediction)* Read the title, and look at the family in the picture. Ask the children to say which one they think is Maya. Ask: *Who do you think is her mum, dad, grandma, brother and sister?* Look at the back cover to find a picture of Maya. Ask: *Were you right?*

C *(Questioning)* Read the questions on the back cover. Answer the questions by looking at the picture on the front cover.

C *(Imagining)* Ask the children to suggest what the names of the other children might be.

Strategy check

Remind the children to read from left to right, and to find and read the sentences in the speech bubbles.

Independent reading

● Ask the children to read the book aloud. Praise and encourage them while they read, and prompt as necessary.

C *(Summarising)* Ask children to tell you what they have found out about Maya's family.

Assessment Check that children:

● (R, AF1) track text from left to right, pointing to each word as they read it

● (R, AF1) use phonic knowledge to sound out and blend the phonemes in words, particularly the phonic words (see chart on page 4)

● (R, AF2) use comprehension skills to talk about the information in the book.

Returning to the text

C (*Questioning, Clarifying*) Ask: *How many people are in Maya's family? Is that the same as your family? Do you have a brother and a sister, just like Maya? What do you have?*

C (*Questioning*) Ask: *How old do you think Maya is? Do you think her brother is older or younger than she is? Is her sister older or younger than she is? Why do you think that?*

C (*Summarising*) Ask the children if they noticed what was the same on every page.

Group and independent reading activities

Objective Hear and say sounds in words in the order in which they occur (5.5).

W Ask the children to say the phonemes in 'mum' and 'dad', separating them out and counting the phonemes with their fingers as they say them. Then remind them how to blend phonemes to make the word. Say the phonemes in the word 'sister' together (s–i–s–t–er). Segment the sounds again, then blend them to make the word. Repeat with 'family'. Praise children for being able to separate out and then blend the sounds.

Assessment (*R, AF1*) Could the children hear and say the separate sounds in 'sister' and 'family'?

Objective Read some high frequency words (5.9).

W Ask the children to tell you the words that you can find on every page: 'This', 'is'. Look for more words that are on nearly every page: 'I', 'am', 'her'. Make some cards with these high frequency words, plus: 'Maya', 'brother', 'sister', 'dad', 'mum', 'grandma'. Ask the children to rearrange the words into different sentences, e.g. *I am her brother*, *This is her sister*, etc. Practise reading the high frequency words out of context, so that the children can read them on sight confidently.

Assessment (*R, AF1*) Could the children read the high frequency words on sight?

Objective Use phonic knowledge to write simple regular words (5.10).

W Ask children how to spell the word 'dad'. Write it on a board. Make a list of the letters: *b h l m p s*. Ask the children to choose any of the letters from the list to change the first letter of 'dad'. Ask: *Can you say and write the new word?* Use all the letters in the list to make new words.

Assessment *(R, AF1)* Can the children write and read the words they have made?

Objective Extend their vocabulary, exploring the meanings and sounds of new words (7.2).

C *(Questioning, Clarifying)* Ask: *What family words can we find in this book?* Make a list starting: mum, dad, etc. Ask the children to think of some more words they know for family members, e.g. 'grandpa', 'aunt', 'nephew', etc. Talk about each new word so that children understand the relationship. Ask the children to tell you about relations they see frequently. If someone mentions an uncle, explain that the child is that uncle's nephew or niece. Explore as many new family words as the children can understand. Some may introduce words such as 'step-dad', or 'great grandma'.

Assessment *(R, AF2)* Could the children understand and use family relationship words?

E-links

E-Fireflies

This book is available electronically, on *e-Fireflies* Stages 1+–2 CD-ROM. You can use 'Explore a Book' with the children, to help them access screens/pages in different orders and annotate the text using the e-tools. You then have a choice of activities to give the children, which will include a sequencing, matching or writing activity.

Use the Teacher Settings screen to select how you want any part of the CD-ROM to be used, and the Progress Report Chart to track the progress of individual children.

Speaking and listening activities

Objective Speak clearly and audibly with confidence and control and show awareness of the listener (1.4).

● Have the children sitting in a circle, and ask them to speak in turn. Ask them to complete the sentence: 'At home I have…' listing family members. Ask them to use family words such as brother, sister, etc. Encourage other children to ask questions such as 'What is your brother called?', 'How old is your baby sister?', etc. Praise children for speaking clearly, and for listening to each other speak.

Cross-curricular links: Early Years Foundation Stage

Personal, Social and Emotional Development

● Understand that people have different needs, cultures, values and beliefs, which need to be treated with respect.

Knowledge and Understanding of the World

● Look closely at similarities, differences, patterns and change.

● Find out about past and present events in their own lives, and in those of their families and other people they know.

Writing activities

Objective Write own names/labels/captions, etc., begin to form simple sentences using some punctuation (11).

● Read the title again. Ask the children to find the word 'Maya' on each page. Ask them to say why there is always a capital 'M'. Ask the children to write their own names, remembering to use a capital letter. Then ask them to draw their family. Ask them to use page 8 of the book to help them to write 'This is my family.' You could develop this by asking children to draw and write a page about each family member and create a book for each child like 'Maya's family'.

Assessment (W, AF2) Can children write their own names unaided? Are they using their knowledge of letter–sound correspondence to write the other words?

Making Muffins

> **C** = Language comprehension
> **W** = Word recognition
>
> **R, AF** = QCA reading assessment focus
> **W, AF** = QCA writing assessment focus

Group or guided reading

Introducing the book

C *(Clarifying)* Look at the picture and ask the children to say what is on the plate. If the children say 'cakes', explain that these cakes are called muffins. Read the title together.

C *(Prediction)* Read the blurb on the back cover and ask the children to say what they think will be inside the book. Use the words 'instructions' and 'recipe'. Look at some of the pages to check that they are right.

Strategy check

Remind the children to use letter sounds and the illustrations to work out new words.

Independent reading

- Ask children to read the book aloud. Praise and encourage them while they read, and prompt as necessary.

C *(Summarising)* Ask the children to tell you what happens on page 8. Talk about why the mother is putting the muffins in the oven.

Assessment Check that children:

- *(R, AF1)* use letter sounds to help them to work out new words
- *(R, AF1)* recognise repeated high frequency words on sight
- *(R, AF2)* use comprehension skills to work out and talk about what is happening.

Returning to the text

C *(Questioning)* Ask: *What did the boy put in first? Can you guess what baking powder is for?*

C *(Clarifying)* Ask children to explain why you need sugar in the muffins. Ask: *Why did the boy put in cocoa?*

C *(Clarifying)* Ask children to explain why the muffins have to go into the oven.

Group and independent reading activities

Objective Read simple words by sounding out and blending from left to right (5.6).

W Ask the children to say all the phonemes of 'muffins' with you (m–u–ff–i–n–s). Blend the sounds to make the words. Ask the children to repeat this, segmenting and blending without your help if possible. Ask them to find the word 'chips' on page 5. Ask them to say all the phonemes, then blend them to read 'chips'. On pages 6 and 7, segment and then blend the phonemes in 'eggs' and 'milk'. Finally, on page 8, ask them to say all the sounds in 'muffins' again and blend them. Praise the children for knowing how to do this.

Assessment *(R, AF1)* Could the children hear and say the separate sounds in these words, then blend them to make the word?

Objective Read some high frequency words (5.9).

W **You will need** word cards for each child with: 'I', 'put', 'in', 'the', 'milk', 'eggs'. Ask the children to tell you which words are on all the pages except page 8: 'I', 'put', 'in', 'the'. Ask them to find particular words on different pages, e.g. *Look at page 7. Can you find 'the'?* Give each child a set of word cards and ask them to make a sentence. Can they change one word and make a different sentence? Ask each child to read the sentence they have made.

Assessment *(R, AF1)* Could the children read the high frequency words on sight, and arrange the words to make and read a sentence?

Objective Show understanding of how information can be found in non-fiction texts (7.3).

C *(Clarifying)* Talk about the ingredients, or what you need, for making muffins. When the children suggest an item, e.g. 'milk', ask them to find that page in the book. Look at the page and ask them to find the word twice, once in the sentence and once on the label in the photograph. (NB There is no label for eggs.) Ask: *Which ingredients look a bit alike?* (sugar, flour, baking powder) Ask the children to explain why labels are useful in this case. Notice that the label word begins with a capital letter in each case.

Assessment *(R, AF2)* Could the children find and read the labels? Did they understand why labels are useful?

Objective Show understanding of how information can be found in non-fiction texts (7.3).

C *(Imagining)* Ask: *What did these muffins taste of? How do you know that?* Ask them to find the page that shows what flavour the muffins were. Ask the children to say what food flavours they like best. Ask them to think of other flavourings for muffins, e.g. orange, lemon, vanilla, ginger. Ask the children to say what ingredients would be necessary for the flavours they choose. Ask them if they know what you would use, e.g. lemon: juice and zest (fine peel); ginger: ground ginger powder.

Assessment *(R, AF2)* Could the children imagine other flavours and say what they would add to the mixture to get those flavours?

E-links

E-Fireflies

This book is available electronically, on *e-Fireflies* Stages 1+–2 CD-ROM. You can read the text as a 'Talking Book' on a whiteboard with the whole class, or on a computer with a group of children. Use the tools to annotate the text with the children. The children can then use 'Make a Book' to select their own choice of content and make their own books.

Use the Teacher Settings screen to select how you want any part of the CD-ROM to be used, and the Progress Report Chart to track the progress of individual children.

Speaking and listening activities

Objective Sustain attentive listening, responding to what they have heard by relevant comments (2.2).

- Make a fun cake. Have a bowl and wooden spoon if possible. Pass the bowl and spoon around the circle and ask the children to say: 'I am making a cake and I put in…'. Each person must add something that has not been mentioned before. It does not need to be realistic for a cake, e.g. 'I put in sausages', but each item should be a kind of food. If children are able to remember previous suggestions they can repeat all the ingredients so far: 'I am making a cake and I put in flour, eggs, sausages, pepper…'.

Cross-curricular links: Early Years Foundation Stage

- **Knowledge and Understanding of the World**

  Investigate objects and materials by using all their senses.

  Ask questions about why things happen and how things work.

Writing activities

Objective Write own names/labels/captions, etc., begin to form simple sentences using some punctuation (11).

- Ask the children to tell you what went into the mixing bowl first. Make a numbered list on a board or large piece of paper, e.g. '1. flour'. Use the book if necessary to continue the list in the right order. Where the words are easy to spell using sounds in sequence, ask the children to tell you how to write the words, e.g. 'eggs', 'milk', 'chips'.

- Ask the children to use the book to illustrate different stages in mixing the cake. Ask them to write: 'He put in…' and copy the ingredient to match their picture. Remind them to begin the sentence with a capital letter and finish with a full stop. Put the pages in sequence and encourage the children to read their own class book.

Assessment *(W, AF2)* Were the children able to locate the ingredients in order? Could they draw one stage and write a simple sentence with help?

Big and Little

> **C** = Language comprehension   *R, AF* = QCA reading assessment focus
>
> **W** = Word recognition   *W, AF* = QCA writing assessment focus

Group or guided reading

Introducing the book

C *(Clarifying)* Read the title, noticing that 'Big' is in big letters and 'Little' is in small letters. Ask the children to say why they think this has been done.

C *(Clarifying)* Ask: *What do you think these black shapes are? Which one is big, and which one is little?*

C *(Prediction)* Read the blurb on the back cover. Ask the children to predict which big animals might be in the book. Ask: *Can you think of little animals that might be in this book?*

Strategy check

Remind the children to point to each word as they read.

Independent reading

● Ask children to read the book aloud. Praise and encourage them while they read, and prompt as necessary.

C *(Summarising)* Ask children to tell you some of the big animals in the book, and the names of some little animals they have read about.

Assessment Check that children:

● *(R, AF1)* match printed word to word read with one-to-one correspondence

● *(R, AF1)* use phonic knowledge to sound out and blend the phonemes in words, particularly the phonic words (see chart on page 4)

● *(R, AF2)* use comprehension skills to understand and compare the sizes of the animals.

Returning to the text

C *(Questioning, Clarifying)* Ask: *Which is bigger, an elephant or a frog?* Ask the children to show you the photographs in the book.

C *(Imagining)* Ask children to think of a very big animal and a very small animal that could be in this book.

C *(Summarising)* Ask the children to explain the shapes on page 8. Ask: *What do these shapes show us? Which is the biggest animal here? Which is the smallest animal here?*

Group and independent reading activities

Objective Link sounds and letters, naming and sounding letters (5.2).

W Look at the first letter of 'rhinoceros'. Ask the children to say the letter name and the sound. Say 'rhinoceros' together. Ask the children if they can hear another 'r' sound in the word. Look for another letter 'r'. Say the word again, stressing the 'r' sound each time. Look at the word 'elephant' in the same way. Notice the 'e' sound at the beginning, then the second 'e' sound. Say the word so that both 'e' sounds can be clearly heard.

Assessment *(R, AF1)* Could the children identify the initial sound in these words? Could they hear the second sound within the word?

Objective Hear and say sounds in the order in which they occur (5.5).

W Ask the children to say the sounds in 'big', then blend them to make the word. Repeat with 'and' and 'frog'. Give plenty of praise if they can do this without help. Find the page that has a parrot. Ask the children to say each phoneme with you in order (p–a–rr–o–t), then blend the sounds to say the word. Think of more animal names that have phonemes the children recognise, e.g. 'fish', 'rabbit', 'robin', 'slug', 'fox'. Make a list. Ask the children to use phonemes to spell each word for you to write.

Assessment *(R, AF1)* Were the children able to hear and say the sounds in order? Could they blend them to say the word?

Objective Read some high frequency words (5.9).

(W) You will need four copies of each of the high frequency words in this book ('This', 'is', 'it', 'look', 'big', 'little', 'at') on pieces of card. Place all the cards face down. Take turns to turn over two cards. The child reads the two words. If they are the same the child keeps them, if not the cards are replaced face down. Continue playing until all the cards have been picked up. The person with most cards wins.

Assessment *(R, AF1)* Could the children read all the words on sight?

Objective Extend their vocabulary, exploring the meanings and sounds of new words (7.2).

(C) *(Questioning)* Ask the children to find all the names of big animals in the book. Talk about each one in turn and allow the children time to say what they know about them. Discuss where the animal lives, what it eats, and whether the children have seen one or not. Ask them to think of some more big animals that they know about, e.g. hippopotamus, polar bear, whale, etc. Then talk about the small animals in the book. Find out what they know about these, and ask them to name more small animals.

Assessment *(R, AF2)* Can the children talk about the animals in the book, and suggest the names of more big and small animals?

E-links

E-Fireflies

This book is available electronically, on *e-Fireflies* Stages 1+–2 CD-ROM. You can read the text as a 'Talking Book' on a whiteboard with the whole class, or on a computer with a group of children. Use the tools to annotate the text with the children. The children can then use 'Make a Book' to select their own choice of content and make their own books.

Use the Teacher Settings screen to select how you want any part of the CD-ROM to be used, and the Progress Report Chart to track the progress of individual children.

Speaking and listening activities

Objective Interact with others, negotiating plans and activities and taking turns in conversation (3.1).

● Provide some small plastic animals or small pictures of animals for the children to sort out. Ask them to work in groups of two or three. Give them a chart like the one on page 8, divided into 'Big' and 'Little'. Ask the children to talk to each other to decide where each animal should go. When they have finished sorting the animals, ask them to give their reasons for placing particular animals. Did everyone agree?

Cross-curricular links: Early Years Foundation Stage

● **Problem Solving, Reasoning and Numeracy**

Use language such as 'bigger' to describe the shape and size of solids and flat shapes.

● **Knowledge and Understanding of the World**

Find out about, and identify, features of living things.
Look closely at similarities, differences, patterns and change.

Writing activities

Objective Attempt writing for various purposes, using features of different forms such as lists (9).

Ask the children to help you to write the alphabet as a list on a long piece of paper. Ask them to think of an animal. Ask the child to tell you the letter that the animal name begins with. Write the word beside the right letter, or help the child to do so. Display the list on the wall, and as children think of or discover new animal names they can be added to the list. Try to complete your animal alphabet.

Assessment (W, AF8) Could the children match the word to the letter of the alphabet and create a list?

Oxford Reading Tree resources at this level

Biff, Chip and Kipper
Stage1+ Patterned Stories
Stage1+ More Patterned Stories A
Stage1+ First Sentences
Stage1+ More First Sentences A
Stage1+ More First Sentences B

Phonics
Stage 1+ Songbirds
Stage 1+ First Phonics
Stage 1+ Floppy's Phonics

Poetry
Glow-worms Stages 1+–2

Non-fiction
Stage 1+ Fireflies
Stage 1+ More Fireflies

Wider reading
Stage 1+ Snapdragons

Electronic
Stage 1/1+ Talking Stories
Stage1+ First Phonics Talking Stories
Stage 1+ for Clicker

e-Songbirds
e-Fireflies
MagicPage
Clip Art
ORT Online www.OxfordReadingTree.com

Teachers' Resources
Sequencing Cards
Comprehension Photocopy Masters
(Stages 1–2)
Context Cards
Teacher's Handbook (Stages 1–9)
Group Activity Sheets
Phonics and Spelling Activities (Stages 1–9)
Stage 1+ Workbooks
Stage 1/1+ Storytapes
Songbirds Teaching Notes, Guided Reading Cards and Parent Notes
Snapdragons Teaching Notes, Guided Reading Cards and Parent Notes
Fireflies Teaching Notes

OXFORD
UNIVERSITY PRESS

Great Clarendon Street, Oxford OX2 6DP

Oxford University Press is a department of the University of Oxford. It furthers the University's objective of excellence in research, scholarship, and education by publishing worldwide in

Oxford   New York

Auckland   Cape Town   Dar es Salaam   Hong Kong   Karachi
Kuala Lumpur   Madrid   Melbourne   Mexico City   Nairobi
New Delhi   Shanghai   Taipei   Toronto

With offices in

Argentina   Austria   Brazil   Chile   Czech Republic   France
Greece   Guatemala   Hungary   Italy   Japan   Poland
Portugal   Singapore   South Korea   Switzerland
Thailand   Turkey   Ukraine   Vietnam

Oxford is a registered trade mark of Oxford University Press
in the UK and in certain other countries

Text © Oxford University Press 2008

Written by Thelma Page

The moral rights of the author have been asserted
Database right Oxford University Press (maker)

First published 2008

British Library Cataloguing in Publication Data

Data available

ISBN: 978-0-19-847260-5

10 9 8 7 6 5 4 3

Page make-up by Thomson Digital

Printed in China

Paper used in the production of this book is a natural, recyclable product made from wood grown in sustainable forests. The manufacturing process conforms to the environmental regulations of the country of origin.